D1310072

THE OHANA WAY FUNDAMENTALS

An Introduction to The Ohana Way

30th Anniversary Edition

By Scot Conway, Ph.D., J.D.

THE OHANA WAY FUNDAMENTALS
An Introduction to The Ohana Way
30th Anniversary Edition

TABLE OF CONTENTS

PROLOGUE

June 12, 1945, and World War 2 was still going on. On that day Sheila Kiyoko Arakawa born on the Big Island in Hawaii. She would grow up on the island. She'd be on her own at the age of 12, working as a live-in domestic. In 1959, she'd celebrate Hawaii becoming the 50th of the United States. In 1965, she'd be back in the hospital she was born in, ready to give birth to her own child, me.

When my father, Gary Conway, couldn't find work in Hawaii, my family relocated back to where he had grown up – San Diego, California. My Hawaii-girl mother would arrange for us to have Ohana in our elementary-school neighborhood. In our diverse neighborhood, all the adults were Aunt and Uncle. Ohana rules governed. Parents can do that for kids at that age.

We moved to a new neighborhood. My mother tried to build ohana again. The families were gathered together, and all the kids met in a neighborhood car pool. It didn't quite work, though. We were friendly enough, but we didn't quite connect. I got to close to one – only one. There was something about the shift from being parent-referenced in elementary school to being peer-referenced as we became teens.

I remember 7th grade. I came home with a perfect report card. Back then, it was straight-As and straight-Es – perfect. There's a "thing" among Asians that jokes about how grades are viewed, the "Asian-F" is a B. My mother saw my report card and sat me down for a conversation. She was concerned. "You're book smart, Scot, but you need to be life smart." She told me she'd rather have a B-student kid with a social life than an A-student kid with the life I'd been living.

It might have been eighth or ninth grade when I started to come out of my shell to assume a new level of social leadership. In High School there was a spot on campus called Henry's Hut. A circle of new friends would gather there before school, after school, and during both lunch periods. By the time I graduated, the group had grown to about 70 people. I remember one day deciding on Wednesday to have a party on Friday, and we had all 70 at my home in two days. Then we graduated.

I tried again in college. Lord knows I was involved. I was a member of several clubs, an officer in some of them, and I applied for a lot of other positions in leadership and on teams. I just didn't seem to manage to build another ohana like in high school. Maybe it had something to do with us being more socially-referenced by then. After all, ohana was a Hawaii-thing, not a Mainland thing.

I built one in a gaming group. It lasted years, but slowly dissolved. I didn't have the vocabulary. I didn't have a way to define quite what I was after. Until I realized that answer had been in my hands since 1971.

It was in 1971 that I took my first martial arts lesson. In 1990, I started what is now known as Guardian Kempo Kajuko Do. I would try to codify a lot more than a physical martial art. I would try to codify a dream. I would, among many other things I'd work on, try to codify Ohana.

The Ohana Way 2.0 is my 30th Anniversary Edition of The Ohana Way in honor of the 1990 start.

The lessons I used to do in my classes, and the things I'd teach my clients – were eventually published in a report and eventually published in a book.

In the early days, I'd just write it out on a white board and teach it in the room. Then it became a report, and I'd email a pdf or print them up in the office and hand them to clients. In time, the 5x5 got fleshed out more and more – particularly on what else I needed to include in it. After a while, I had most of a book already written, so it was just a matter of organizing my notes and getting it done.

Originally, it was just intended for my clients. I could not guess how many copies of the report and book I've handed out, had downloaded, or otherwise given to people. It was 2017 when The Ohana Way came to the attention of the business world… and now here we are.

After some experience teaching outside my usual circles… it was time to update. I found some of the follow-up lessons people found most profound included some things I thought were worth introducing at this level, and I re-sequenced some of the material. After all, most of the people I worked with before had a relationship with me and everything they read either already had a context – or shortly would. It became clearer that for an audience that didn't already have that relationship and might not develop it shortly, I might want to bring it to them a little differently.

To improve the experience for you, the reader, The Ohana Way 2.0… in celebration of 30 years.

Welcome to the celebration.

CHAPTER ZERO

HOW TO READ THIS BOOK

This book is meant to be easy reading.

It's short enough to be read in one or two sittings. The writing is intended to be straightforward and easy to understand. It's organized simply so you can come back to it any time and find the part you're looking for.

Some of the ideas may seem obvious. Others will be profound and might even be a little mind-bending. Those ideas might be a little more challenging to wrap your head around. It's worth it! What may be obvious to you might be mind-bending to someone else, and the same is true is reverse.

In our experience, everyone already does some of what you'll find in this book. Also based upon our experience, many aspects are brand new to a lot of people.

THE TRIPLE-TOUCH TECHNIQUE

Get the most out of this book using the Triple-Touch Technique.

1. Awareness
2. Light Attention
3. Focused Attention

Level One: Awareness – See Every Page.

Flip through every single page. Spend about one second on each page. Take a look at the Table of Contents, look at the chapter headings, and glance at section headings and other parts that stand out to you.

Just spend a few minutes with the book and set it aside. If you want to get to it right away, just leave it aside for twenty minutes. Otherwise, it's best to glance at it either at night just before bed or in the morning just after waking. Then get to it later in the day or sometime the next day.

What you're doing is letting your brain form a "mental filing cabinet" for the material. Your brain has seen what's in the book so it knows what to expect. It sets up a loose structure ready to be filled with the information it knows to expect.

Level Two: Light Attention – Look and Read a Little.

Now you'll invest a bit more time. Read the Table of Contents. Reading it aloud is powerful for a lot of reasons. Really read the chapter headings, the section headings, and anything else that grabs your attention. Read the Chapter Summaries.

Level Three: Focused Attention – Read.

You can read it all in one sitting if you like. It's organized to start simply and then dive deeper. The opening sections introduce ohana as a concept and then give a very surface-insight into it.

Then the sections for each element of OHANA follow. You can read just one of "the five" and ponder it for that day. Or you could read all five of them. That's up to you.

Activation: Repeat Level One or Level Two, as desired.

Whenever you want to refresh your attention, go back through the book again at Level One. This should only take a few minutes. Just flip through the pages and mentally note if the ideas there are familiar to you.

If you feel it's gotten fuzzy in your mind, do Level Two. Re-read the Chapter Summaries. Use bookmarks to hold the places you might want to go back to and read again. Re-read any section about which you might want to think about more deeply.

That's the process of reading the book. It's actually exactly the same technique we teach to high school and college students for studying their textbooks. This system lets you increase your retention with very little adjustment in your strategy! Feel free to use it with any reading material.

UNDERSTAND WHAT WE MEAN

The way we use language to describe things may be a little different than how you might use the same words. It's certainly more specific than many people experience. We try to define our terms as we go.

It's totally okay if you don't use our vocabulary the exact same way we do. Just learn the idea. Call it whatever you want in your own life. Just know that we use words to mean certain things. When we use those words, we mean those certain things.

Just let us mean what we mean. In time, the little bit of extra precision of our vocabulary with pretty clean definitions lets us all be on the same page. That way we're not getting lost arguing over words when what we're really after is ideas!

IT IS ABOUT ME; IT IS NOT ABOUT "THEM"

When we read about new ideas, it's very natural to read and think, "Yeah, so-and-so needs to know this!" Or we might think, "I wish my parents did this for me when I was a kid!"

Basically, it's easy to see what other people should do differently. It's easy to see what other people should have known or should have done better. Other people are who they are. They do what they do. By reading a book or attending a seminar, my new learning doesn't change who they are or what they did.

It CAN change me, though! So that's my focus.

I look for what I can learn. I look for what I can do better. I look for where I can be a better example.

I go first. I *grow* first.

I make sure I understand first. If I can share some helpful ideas in a way that illuminates, that can be helpful. It's part of "Be a light, not a judge" and "be a safe person."

Depending upon our relationship, the best we might do is be a better example. Then we can explain the example we're being.

My job is to BE Ohana.

If there are ten of us, each of us waiting for everyone else to go first, no one is going. If there are ten of us, each of us practicing Ohana, then every one of us has nine people doing for us! So, we just go first. We ALL go first.

We walk the path. We SHOW others the way. We don't just TELL them; we SHOW them. That's the basic definition of "sensei," that senior person who teaches because they did it first.

ENJOY THE ADVENTURE

OHANA can be absolutely transformational. Parts of Ohana might be the exact opposite of how you grew up. Bits might be very, very different from what your life looks like right now. If this is true, there is a good chance you have years of training and practice doing things a way you now want to change.

You'll also find that parts are exactly how you do it – or very close. Those parts will give you a vocabulary to discuss it with others.

Whether you're making tiny adjustments or huge changes, enjoy the process. It's an adventure! All of us have experiences and insights as we go through life. That changes us. Since we're going to change anyway, we may as well change on purpose! Then we can pick a direction that we really like! Ohana is one of those great directions.

Enjoy the adventure to the OHANA Ideal!

CHAPTER ZERO SUMMARY

1. Triple Touch Technique
   Awareness – Look at Every Page.
   Light Attention – Look and Read a Little.
   Focused Attention – Read.

   Activate

2. Understand What We Mean

3. It is About ME; It is Not About Them.

4. Enjoy the Adventure!

CHAPTER ONE

OHANA INTRODUCTION

"Ohana means family. Family means no one gets left behind or forgotten." – Lilo and Stitch

Thanks to the movie Lilo and Stitch, popular culture has a basic definition of ohana. The movie came out in 2002, and children born many years after still know the definition of ohana from the movie. Such is the power of Disney. I sat down with five and six year-olds, and when I ask them if they know what ohana means, they do. They have the Disney definition down perfect!

The definition really is pretty good. In the movie, ohana includes Lilo and her sister Nani. Stitch is adopted as ohana, which drives much of the story. Over the course of the series, ohana includes David, Jumba, Pleakley, and all the other 625 experiments. It illustrates that ohana goes way beyond those you're related to by blood or marriage. It's those you're "related to" because of love.

"Calabash cousin" is part of ohana. This Hawaiian custom (and by no means unique to Hawaii) is that close friends become cousins. Older men and women are often auntie or uncle. "Family" is a bond of blood and marriage, of course, and good friends also become family.

While you definitely find this extended, deeper meaning of family in Hawaii, you find it in many other places. In contemporary mainland culture, the *Fast and Furious* series of movies uses a similar concept. Dominic Toretto (Vin Diesel) says to Deckard Shaw (Jason Statham), "I don't have friends; I got family." (*Furious 7*, 2015). "Family" is more than blood for a lot of people.

Many of us grew up considering some of our best friends as brothers and sisters. Some of us grew up calling our friends' mothers "mom." We all understand that people consider friends we consider more than friends. They can become family. We use phrases like "brother from another mother" and "sister from another mister."

With Ohana, "real" relationships trump "legal" relationships. You can search back through blood and marriage and find the common ancestor and you're legally related. With Ohana, you can be cousins without any regard to whether you actually related. Some cousins may or may not be related. They don't know. They don't care. They're cousins no matter what.

At the Guardian Quest Dojo, anyone can show up and take lessons.

Becoming part of the family is optional.

Some do. Some don't.

I wanted to be the person I wished I had in my life when I was young. I wanted to teach my students the things I wished I had learned. I actually did learn a lot of it when I was young. Most of it came later.

My mother became a grandmother. With "grandmother's eyes" she saw things she had not seen as a mother. She saw that some things were critically important that she hadn't given much attention. She saw that other things weren't nearly as big a deal as she thought. We were close enough that I got the benefit of her new insights and realizations.

So I showed up with "grandfather eyes" to teach.

As a master of martial arts, I started off with an assumption that everyone who came wanted to learn the physical art of protecting oneself and others. When my students had to use their skill and successfully stopped criminal after criminal, I thought, "I am doing my job." We had a great art with powerful techniques. We taught well and our students learned.

In the first 25 years of me teaching, we tallied 30 criminal assaults against my students, with 30 successful defenses. Yes, a lot of that is skill. I readily admit that a lot of it is luck, too. When a particular white belt learned a defense against a punch, and two weeks later the criminal that attacks punches at him, that's luck.

As it turns out, that's only one small part of my job. Only about one-in-three people ever gets targeted with violence at a level where they need that kind of self-protection skill. Those that face violence more often are usually in a dangerous environment: a particularly bad neighborhood, a dangerous job, or an abusive relationship. The majority of people manage to get through their whole lives without ever being seriously attacked (serious defined as requiring medical attention afterwards).

Another part of my job is transformation. I knew that. I teach a "lifestyle martial art," meaning it's more about teaching people how to live than it is how to fight.

A long, long time ago I learned this concept: "A good teacher will show you how to fight; a great teacher will show you how to live." There's an incredible amount of transformational material in what I do. By way of example, some of it is so powerful that it can even teach your body to stop having allergic reactions. I know, crazy stuff!

Here's the big surprise. Over my first quarter century of teaching, the single most common thing that gets said is this: "I love my dojo family."

It's about family. It's about Ohana.

I had no idea how important this would be when I started. In fact, as important as transformation and effective martial arts are, what people crave most is the community we have.

We're open to anyone. Not everyone wants to be a part of the family. That's okay. Some people would rather just train and go home.

Those who become family remain family. There are those who have left us because they got stationed elsewhere, or they moved out of State, or, in some cases, they even moved to another country!

You can tell how important our family is to us and others by the number of people who come visit when they're in town. Sometimes old students get in touch online to ask for the same kind of advice they might seek if they still lived near and trained with us. Some leave for a while and return.

Ohana means family. It means you are more important than just your role. You are more important than just the money paid as a client. You matter as a whole person. You matter. And if you're the type of person who likes that and gives back to others, then you can quickly and easily be ohana, too!

This is our culture. Feel free to adopt any or all of it for your own!

CHAPTER ONE SUMMARY

1. "Ohana means family. Family means no one gets left behind or forgotten." – Lilo and Stitch

2. Calabash Cousin, Auntie, Uncle... "family" as a culture of connection.

3. Real Relationships trump Legal Relationships

4. Grandmother Eyes – See things from a Generational Perspective.

5. Ohana means Family.

6. Adopt Any or All of It for Yourself.

CHAPTER TWO

OHANA

THE FOUNDATION

Here's the really, really short version, right out of a Disney movie:

OHANA – "Ohana means family, and family means no one gets left behind… or forgotten." (*Lilo and Stich*, 2002)

Ohana means family. Family is much more than those related by blood or marriage. It does include them, of course. It also includes friends, calabash cousins, and anyone with whom you share enough in common that you might consider them ohana.

One aspect of this shows up in a simple term: "Hawaii." When people connected to the islands do nice things for one another, they sometimes call it simply "Hawaii." When someone used to live in Hawaii but they have left behind that kind of natural generosity common in the islands, they sometimes say "They aren't Hawaii anymore."

EVERYTHING POSITIVE ABOUT FAMILY

A simple way to think about Ohana is this: It's all the positive things about family. It's all the positive things a family ought to be.

We may agree or disagree on some bits and pieces about what we mean by that – but there's the ideal. Whatever family ought to be… that's Ohana. We will define it more completely as we go… but there's the beginning of it!

Kathleen looked like someone punched her in the gut. She looked half-dazed. Her knees were weak. Something happened. Whatever it was, it was bad.

We didn't know her much more than as a dinner companion on the cruise ship. The ship sat ten to a table. On the first night, we made a game of getting to know everyone's name and who was with whom. Kathleen and her teenaged son, Jim, were two of our eight tablemates.

I asked her what was wrong as a crewmember helped her to a comfortable place to sit down. Kathleen couldn't tell us the whole story herself. She could hardly breathe. With her permission, the crewmember told us what happened.

"Her son didn't make it back to the ship. He's lost in Hilo." No wonder she was almost in shock!

Hilo is the biggest city on the "Big Island" of the State of Hawaii. The cruise ship had put into port that morning and set sail again at 5pm. The next stop was on the far side of the island at 7am the next morning. Somehow, Jim didn't make it back to the ship!

As Kathleen settled herself, she explained that Jim had asked to go shopping. He had money, he knew where the ship was, he knew what he wanted to get and where to go for it. He promised he'd be back early. Against the judgment of her fears, she decided to give her son some extra freedom.

Everything that could be done from aboard ship had been done. In Kona, she planned to disembark and go back to Hilo to find her son. The police had been notified. The cruise line had been notified. The only thing there was left to

22

do was for Kathleen to try to make it through the night and get back to Hilo to find Jim.

The next morning the ship docked in Kona. Kathleen was on the first transfer to the shore. There was already the hustle and bustle of the cruise-ship-in-port activity at the shore. Even so, she saw him there standing on the dock waving. It took an extra moment to make sure her mom-brain wasn't seeing what she had wished for all night.

It was Jim! He had somehow beaten the ship to the other side of the island!

HOW HER SON BEAT US TO THE OTHER SIDE

He got to Kona before the ship did. He made it all the way to the opposite side of the island, fed and rested, and was waiting on the dock for his mother.

How? This was Hawaii!

We later learned that Jim mixed up the departure time in Hilo with the arrival time in Kona. He thought the ship sailed at 7, so he showed up at 6. The ship had already been gone for an hour! The driver, realizing the ship had already sailed, asked if it had been to the other side of the island, yet. He knew that ships put into both ports, so if this was the first stop on the Big Island, it would be on the other side of the island in the morning.

The taxi driver took Jim home to hang out with his own teenaged sons. He let the boy hang out with his family, have dinner with them, and sleep over. In the morning, the boy had breakfast with the family.

In the early morning, the cab driver drove the boy all the way across the island in time to meet the ship when it put into port. The fare would have been hundreds of dollars that the boy did not have, but that didn't matter.

This was Hawaii. A boy had to be reunited with his mother. A family had a cruise to finish. This was a chance for "Hawaii" to shine!

Kathleen had no words for the relief and love that exploded from her heart when she saw Jim. She thanked the cab driver profusely who would not accept any more money for his services. His joy was getting the family back together so they could continue their vacation.

That's Hawaii. That's Ohana.

Someone didn't make it to the ship and got left behind. A Hawaiian family had the ability to get the boy to the ship so he could catch up. No one gets left behind - not if we can help it!

The idea of "no one gets left behind" means you don't get "ditched." It means you don't get kicked out of the group. It means no one becomes the target or the butt of jokes. You're not bullied.

If we extend it to romance, it means no one "ghosts" (what we used to call "dumping") – meaning no one just disappears without at least having a talk about it.

YOU CAN STAY

Of course people get to decide if they want to stay behind. That's different.

"No one gets left behind" does not mean you're not allowed to stay behind. If you don't want to come along, ohana doesn't drag you along against your will.

The exception, of course, is parents with their minor children. Then you might get dragged along, like it or not. If so, you may as well step up your own game. BE ohana. Be part of your family!

For most things, though, coming along or staying behind is a choice you get to make. Ohana won't ditch you. Ohana won't drag you along kicking and screaming either. It's up to you. You're invited.

BEHAVIOR MIGHT HAVE TO GO

Behavior might be kicked out.

Sometimes some people insist on behaving badly. Like a job at which someone does not do the job, either the behavior needs to be upgraded or the person is deciding for themselves to not be part of the team.

It's the same with Ohana. If someone decides that violating the principles is more important to them than the ohana, that's up to them. Ohana will give them a chance. What they do with that chance it up to them.

It's not the person, though. It's the behavior.

Think about this idea: If I need to change a relationship because of a problem I'm having with someone – why? What's the problem? What if there was no problem? If there was no problem, would I be willing to keep that person in that position? Of course! The problem is the problem. The person is not the problem. They may show up together, but the person is not the problem.

This is important to understand. We'll get into it more shortly as we discuss what we call Ohana 101: Hero, Villain, Victim.

NO ONE GETS FORGOTTEN

It's the nature of life that priorities ebb and flow. Life just gets busy sometimes. It's very easy for people to go weeks, months or even years without seeing one another.

Going away to college, being stationed overseas, or moving too far away to visit can interrupt any relationship for some period of time. Sometimes a change in a season of life interrupts and changes relationships. When someone gets married, has a child (or *another* child), starts a new job, or gets involved in any major projects, relationships can be interrupted.

Part of "no one is forgotten" means you can pop back up any time and expect to be just as liked and loved as you were when you left. It helps if you handled your departure well. Remember the "no one gets left behind" means you don't "ghost," you don't just vanish without explanation.

Of course, it's possible that if someone handled their time toward the end of the relationship poorly, that may have done damage. Whatever someone does becomes part of the history of the relationship. That demonstration of what to expect gets factored in the relationship going forward. But you also recognize that people learn and grow. While history might be one of the best ways guess at the future, the past does not equal the future. It might give us cause to tread a bit more cautiously. We can let go of a past and give someone a chance to show they've grown.

Part of "no one is forgotten" means when you show up again, you're always welcomed back. It's the kind of friendship where you can go without seeing a friend for years, but when you visit it's like you never left.

To be honest, it's possible if you've been gone for a while, we might not remember you. That's okay. Just re-introduce yourself, and you're right back in the family. It's easy! That's the way ohana works.

CHAPTER TWO SUMMARY

1. Ohana is all the positive things about family. It's all the positive things a family ought to be.

2. No one is forgotten. No one is ditched. No one ghosts.

3. You can stay behind if you choose.

4. Behavior may have to go.

5. No one is forgotten.

CHAPTER THREE

OHANA 101

HERO, VILLAIN, AND VICTIM

Here's a simple model: Hero, Villain, Victim. I call that Ohana 101. It's easy to see how Ohana works using this model. Let's define the pieces:

> Hero – One who makes it better.
> Villain – One who makes it worse.
> Victim – One for whom it is made worse.

GUARANTEED LACK OF PERFECTION

People are not perfect. In fact, imperfection is one of the few certainties about people – even the best and brightest. We call that a Guaranteed Lack of Perfection.

By definition, that means we will periodically have People Problems. There are a couple of very-common responses to that.

One is to bite your tongue and not say anything. Maybe some passive-aggressive behaviors show up, but the hard conversation is avoided.

Maybe it's avoided just because we don't know how to have it. Maybe it's avoided because we feel we will just keep having the exact same conversation again and again and nothing will ever change anyway.

We might even avoid it because we think the other person will react out-of-proportion to the problem and we just don't want to deal with that. We don't want to be the messenger with a "shoot the messenger" sort of leader.

Another response is to have the hard conversation – and be harsh. This may happen because we're hurt, we're angry, and it's all pouring out of us AT the other person. We tend to blame (it IS their fault, after all), and sometimes we'll argue long and hard to make sure they know and understand that they are the villain and we are the victim.

Then what?

Usually we want them to make it better. We might demand they change. We might manipulate to threaten. Whatever the ultimatum (which we may or may not follow-through on), we're trying to force change.

Maybe we get an agreement – more likely a capitulation from someone who just wants to not be in trouble.

After that... maybe something changes... maybe it doesn't. If it does change, maybe it lasts... or maybe not. Often, we end up repeating the same conversation (argument) again and again until we finally just end the relationship.

No matter how we handle it, what was our ultimate goal?

We wanted something made better.

How did we start? In one, we started with the Victim Frame, and we martyred ourselves. Maybe we hoped something would change by itself... but there was no strategy to get an agreement for change.

In the other we started with the Villain Frame. We cast the other person as the Villain, and we argued for them to be in that role. We demanded they acknowledge it. Why? Because we want them to make it better? Wait... that's the other role....

THE HERO FRAME

The goal is to get them help you make things better. So rather than be their Victim as in the Victim Frame, and rather than case them as the Villain as in the Villain Frame – use the Hero Frame!

Cast them in or recruit them for the role of Hero.

You want to help make things better, right? You want them to help make things better. We want to eliminate the role of Victim... so gather together as a Team Of Heroes to make things better. If things are made better, we no longer have someone for whom they are made worse. We have two Heroes and no Victim!

What about the Villain? Surely we must have a Villain! We do, actually. But the Villain is not a person. The Problem is the Villain. The Problem. Not the person, even if the problem came through or because of the person – the Problem is the Villain.

We are recruiting the person to join us in making things better. We're a team working to solve the problem. We're recruiting a Hero.

HEROES TEAMING UP WITH HEROES

This is Ohana 101. We behave as Heroes – people who make things better.

We look for people to join us as Heroes – being part of making things better.

We externalize what is making things worse. It's the Problem making things worse. The Problem is the Villain, the Person is the Hero.

DO NOT ARGUE FOR A LOSS

"Do not argue for a premise where winning costs you everything you really want."

A simple example is found in Hero, Villain, Victim. If you argue that someone else is the Villain (they make it worse) when your objective is to recruit them to be a Hero (they make it better), winning the Villain-argument is losing. If you convince them that they're the Villain – that it's not the Problem that's the problem – it's THEM – you lose. They have accepted that fundamentally who-they-are is bad and makes things worse.

Now you're trying to get someone with the Identity of "bad" and "worse-making" to now be "good" and "better-making." Can you see how all the energy extended on the argument has been worse than wasted? The goal of Ohana is "everything positive about family."

In particular, if they really are a Villain - if they really do have the identity of a "worse-maker" – then maybe we should have a different relationship with them.

What if they aren't really a Villain? What if it was just a mistake and they really are a "better-maker" – a Hero – exactly what we want them to be… but we argued for them being a Villain? Then aren't we making things worse? We

32

have become the Villain. That's not what we're trying to do, either.

Another version is ascribing negative motives. If someone does not actually have negative motives, then we are the Villain. If they do, then we're arguing for their villainy – maybe even rightly so – in which case why do we have the relationship we have? And people with bad motives rarely agree that they have bad motives.

Rather, we focus on behavior. If someone chooses the behavior themselves – warning us that we should expect more of it in the future – we make our choices based upon that.

We focus our energy on the outcome we desire. We focus our energy on Heroes recruiting Heroes for Hero-work against Problem-Villains. We be Ohana – and we build Ohana.

CHAPTER THREE SUMMARY

1. Ohana 101: Hero, Villain, Victim
    Hero – One who makes it better.
    Villain – One who makes it worse.
    Victim – One for whom it is made worse.

2. Guaranteed Lack of Perfection. We will all mess up. I will. You will. Everyone.

3. The Hero Frame: See People as Heroes and the Villain is the Problem.

4. Ohana 101: Heroes Teaming With Heroes.

5. Do not argue for a proposition where winning means you lose everything that's really important to you.

6. Be Ohana – Build Ohana.

CHAPTER FOUR

SETTLING INTO OHANA

Being Ohana begins with developing an understanding of what we mean. We can start with as simple thing as the Hero, Villain, Victim framework of Ohana 101. When it comes time to do it, we need to embody it.

There are many techniques and tools available that work for this. We'll just take one and build it a little bit here.

A Metaphor for the Ohana Habit

Suppose I teach you a particular martial arts technique, a shoulder lock for example. At first, you'll do it with a training partner who will cooperate with you so you can learn the pieces. In time, you'll start to work with it in the middle of a match. A partner might give you an easy chance to do it and even coach you through it. When you start to get good at it, you can do it in a match.

At first, you might realize only afterwards that you had a chance to use your move. Someone might even have to point it out. In time, you start to see that you just missed your chance. Then you see the opportunity when it's there, maybe in time to try, maybe just a little too late. Eventually, you see it coming and you can apply your move because you see the opportunity as it approaches. You also learn to create the opportunity.

Ohana can be a lot like that. You learn. You apply. You miss your chance. You get better at catching yourself. In time, it becomes a habit and you see your opportunity to do it coming – and you do it.

It takes time to develop the kind of skill to do it automatically. If you take a moment beforehand to get centered, you can do it right nearly every time.

PAUSE, PREPARE, PROCEED, PRACTICE

In many martial arts, there's a simple protocol when entering the dojo or stepping on to the mat: You pause, bow, and then enter. In the art I teach, we break it down into four steps: Pause, Prepare, Proceed, Practice.

When you know you will need to have a conversation or other interaction, take a moment to follow these four steps. The more important the relationship, the more important it is to be consistent with the steps. In time, they happen automatically unless something specifically derails you.

In particular, when you already know you have a meeting of any kind and may need to be at your very best, take a moment – even just ten seconds or a minute – and get centered.

Pause. Stop for a moment. Mentally separate yourself from distractions, especially the kind of distractions that might off-balance you.

Prepare. Think of whatever framework you're using. If you're reading through this for the first time, you might settle into the framework of "family," no gets left behind, or no one is forgotten - and think of what that means in this moment.

You might use the Hero Frame and think about allying with the person and keeping yourself clear that the only villain here is the problem itself.

If you're using the full Ohana Five, you might give yourself a few seconds on each of Ohana: Oasis, Harmony, Assertiveness, Nobility, and Aloha. Here, and most certainly if you're using some portion of the Ohana 5x5, you might want to refer to a printed list. If you have the Ohana Two-Page, take a look at it. Read it over. Settle on the particular pieces you might need the most.

Proceed. Once you feel settled, hopefully somewhere in the range of seconds to a minute, then move forward. Proceed in martial arts often means entering the dojo or stepping onto the training floor. Here, it might mean calling someone into your office or entering theirs. It might mean going to or walking into the meeting room, or logging into it if it's online. Proceed when you're ready.

Practice. Carry the sense of what you're doing with you, and seek to embody it, demonstrate it, and apply it to the moment at hand.

Take Your Time, Then Speed Up

When I'm teaching a new martial arts skill or combination, I ask for the students to go slow and easy. What I'm after is "mechanical exactness." The easy version of that? Do it well. Speed up later.

With Ohana, as we Pause and Prepare, the simple goal is to do it well. At first, especially if you're angry or frustrated, you might have to take more time here. You might want to insert some other technique into with the Pause or Prepare slot. I certainly have a lot of tools I use for myself or clients. If you already know any, you can use them here.

When you're doing it well, then work at doing it well faster. Develop a pattern of investing about a minute each time. When you do as much as you choose in about a minute, then do it faster. For myself, I'll typically spend about ten seconds making sure I'm settled into the right frame of mind – framework – before I step into a situation where I'll need a proper mental state.

CHAPTER FOUR SUMMARY

1. Settle into Ohana.

2. Metaphor: Martial Arts
   Learn
   Apply
   See the opportunity pass you by
   See it while it's here
   See it coming

3. Pause, Prepare, Proceed, Practice
   Pause. Stop and disconnect from distractions.
   Prepare. Settle into the Ohana Frame you'll be using.
   Proceed. When you're settled, move forward to start
your meeting.
   Practice. Embody, demonstrate and apply the Ohana
Frame.

4. Take Your Time, Then Speed Up
   Pause and Prepare as long as you need to do it well.
   When you're doing well, then do it well faster.

CHAPTER FIVE

O.H.A.N.A.

"I knew I'd feel better as soon as I got here... and I do."

Brielle worked and went to school. Her days were often long and sometimes exhausting. This particular day was bad. School was hard. She failed a test in a class required for her major.

Work was terrible. A vulgar customer hit on her and nothing polite she said was getting him to stop. Another customer yelled at her for what turned out to have been the customer's own mistake.

It was one of those days when life just piled on and kept piling on. She recently was sick on top of it. "Probably all the stress" she concluded. Physically, she just wanted to go home and go to bed. Home had stresses of its own. She wasn't in a hurry to get there.

She needed her ohana. She raced to where they were. As she walked in the door, she could almost feel the stress being peeled off her back. It fell to the ground outside to sink away.

Brielle was with people who she knew were her partners. She knew she was with this special family she had chosen.

O.H.A.N.A.

Ohana means family. Family includes those bonded by affection and something in common.

It represents an ideal that we illustrate by using ohana as an acronym. Technically, that means we should always have periods between our letters as in O.H.A.N.A., but we often dispense with the periods and just write it OHANA or even just capitalize Ohana. This way we know we're talking about our five-part acronym.

OHANA means:

O-Oasis
H-Harmony
A-Assertiveness
N-Nobility
A-Aloha

Each one of these elements has a more complete, deeper expression than this (which we explore in future chapters). As a starting place, this is what we mean:

OASIS – Be a Refreshing Refuge. Being an Oasis and helping create an Ohana Oasis means I always make it better by being here. I help create a refuge from the usual, the annoying and the difficult.

HARMONY – Embrace Infinite Diversity in Infinite Combinations Aimed at Greatness. Great music is made from melody and harmony. Many instruments, notes, and singers work together to make all sorts of different and amazing music. Harmony means we don't have to be alike to be together.

ASSERTIVENESS – Moving Forward on Purpose with Respect for Others. We Live Life on Purpose. We live assertively, learn assertively and love assertively. We practice assertive listening, assertive relationships, assertive parenting, and assertiveness in any and all areas of life.

NOBILITY – Be our Highest and Best Selves. The metaphor of the Royal Knight dives deep into our ideals of princeliness and princessliness in their highest and best forms. We pursue knightly chivalry and samurai bushido in service to high ideals.

ALOHA – Love in All Its Many Meanings and Manifestations. Love is I want the best for you, I want to be the best for you, and I want you to have transcendent joy. Aloha also includes hello and goodbye in Hawaiian.

OHANA FIVE BY FIVE

Each one of the five larger ideas has within it five ideas that fit the theme. We call this the "Ohana Five By Five."

The term "five by five" means things are the best quality. It comes from radio communication as a sign that the signal was perfectly readable and very strong. Our Ohana Five By Five is meant to be easily read, clearly understood, and very strong for building powerful, positive relationship when applied.

The Ohana Five by Five builds from the five ideals of Ohana: Oasis, Harmony, Assertiveness, Nobility, and Aloha. We'll dive more deeply into each ideal first, and then we'll go into each of the five by five.

Importantly, the Ohana 5x5 is not an instant standard. It would be easily possible to start with the concept of "everything positive 'family' should mean" and the Hero Frame. As you get to the Ohana Five, you're reaching for about the limit of new things people would do all at once.

The Ohana 5x5 is built up over time. With 25 more precise expressions of Ohana, you're not likely to instantly shift all of them all at once. Start with the basics, and focus on the rest of a little at a time. Otherwise it just becomes on giant collection of interesting, useful ideas that it read, applauded, and then left behind – as almost all of us with almost all new things we learn! It's so very, very human.

That means to apply these ideas in real life, we have to be intentional about it. Start off with what they are, and consider which ideas can create a shift in your life, your relationships, your business, or your career right now – and do the ones you can do!

The Ohana Five By Five are:

OASIS
Be a Refreshing Refuge.
>   1:   Leave No Trace; Better Than You Found It
>   2:   Be a Safe Person; Create a Safe Place
>   3:   Give to Givers Who Give
>   4:   Win/Win or No Deal
>   5:   Resolve (My, Your, Our), Concede (Trade Wins), Compromise

HARMONY
Embrace Infinite Diversity in Infinite Combinations Aimed at Greatness.
>   1:   Just Be Polite
>   2:   More For, Less Against. Focus on What You Do Want.
>   3:   Facet Truths: Bring Truth Appropriate to the Relationship
>   4:   Differences are Issues to Navigate, Not Causes for Condemnation

5:      Bad Things are Problems to Solve, Not Causes for Condemnation

ASSERTIVENESS

Moving Forward on Purpose with Respect for Others.

1:      I Have a Point; You May Also Have a Point
2:      More Yes/And, Less No/But
3:      Define Your Win: Values, Goals, and Roles
4:      Compelling Future: Choose. Plan. Check In
5:      Ecology Check

NOBILITY

Royal Knight: Be our highest and best selves.

1:      Language Of Emotions
2:      Be a Light, Not a Judge
3:      Self-Leadership
4:      360 Degree Leadership: 4P360
5:      Living By a Code

ALOHA

Love:

1. I want the best for you.
2. I want to be the best for you.
3. I want you to have transcendent joy.

1:      Love Stack: Agape, Phileo, Eros
2:      Love Is & Love Is Not: A Self-Check
3:      Phileo Bank Account: Positive On Purpose
4:      Love, Joy, Peace; God, People, Self
5:      100 Ways to Win: YORI

CHAPTER FIVE SUMMARY

1. Ohana means family

2. O.H.A.N.A. is an acronym
   Oasis
   Harmony
   Assertiveness
   Nobility
   Aloha

3. The Ohana 5x5 includes 25 more specific expressions of Ohana.

4. Apply the 5x5 a few elements at a time. Start with what will make a difference that you can do – and do that.

CHAPTER SIX

OASIS

Be a Refreshing Refuge.

O-OASIS
H-Harmony
A-Assertiveness
N-Nobility
A-Aloha

The fresh baked chocolate chip cookies didn't actually solve anything – but boy did I feel better.

My mom knew that things were tough, so on that particular day she decided that fresh-baked cookies might help me feel better.

To this day, if I want to feel better, one of the things I still do is bake cookies. I usually find others to share them with since I can't eat that many by myself. I just like the smell of them baking.

Certainly my mom didn't invent the technique. It's so common that real estate agents are trained to have fresh-baked cookies in a home they're showing. So many of us have come home to the fresh-baked cookie smell that we associate it with the best of what "home" is all about.

We call it "life," but, frankly, a lot of "life" really does suck the life out of us. It's like being in a desert. We go through our day-to-day work, our to-do lists, our jobs, our classes, our homework, our tasks, dealing with a mix of nice-people and not-so-nice people... and we need a break.

An oasis, literally, is an area of water and vegetation in the middle of a desert. For those who lived in deserts, knowing the location of an oasis was the difference between living and dying.

Often, life is like a desert. We're out and about in the day-to-day world doing what we must. It can dry out our souls and drain our hearts of strength.

BE A REFRESHING REFUGE

While I was working on this book, an interesting thing happened.

I got a text from a friend who asked if I was available to talk. It was unusual for our contact to be more than casual, so I figured something was going on. We got on the phone and she was in tears.

For the first time in her life, a man had hit her – really hit her – hard. She was shocked, stunned, in physical pain and for the first time she was terrified of a man.

When that happened, she knew one person whom she trusted could help her feel better. Me.

From time to time something like that happens. After all, I'm a martial arts master, so naturally people think of me for protection from violence. What was new was that we were hundreds of miles apart from one another. Obviously, I was too far away to offer any real protection. Yet, I had become so associated with feeling safe, that I was her oasis in the middle of that particular fear.

Can I do anything practical from hundreds of miles away? Of course not. It's all emotion. She just felt safer because she heard my voice. That's Oasis.

So you never know in what way you might have an opportunity to make someone's life better. You never know when you might be just the oasis someone needs.

BETTER BECAUSE YOU'RE HERE

The principle of being Oasis is simple: Make it better because you're here.

There are people who walk into a room like a fresh breeze. They show up and it's just better. Maybe it's as simple a thing as a nice smile, that they acknowledge you as a person. It might be a pat on the shoulder as they walk by. It could be something a little more meaningful like a hug or a kiss – depending upon context.

With some people, just their presence is enough. You might not even talk much, or at all, but knowing this particular person is nearby is comforting.

I'm a martial arts master. So, of course, I get to hear some version of "I sure don't want to make you angry!" comment a lot. The truth of it is almost exactly the opposite of that.

I never did find out who she was, but in response to a recent comment on "you could kick my butt," a young woman had something very different to say.

"You're a karate master? Wow. I feel really safe right now."

That was the whole conversation. She kept on with whatever she was doing, and I continued with what I was doing. She felt better knowing that in the room was someone with more than four decades of training to keep people safe. I felt better knowing that at least one person knew they were safer because I was near.

There are too many people you see that require you brace yourself. They might take out a bad day on you. They might be drunk. They might call you names. They might yell at you, judge you, or make demands. The world already has too many of those. We don't need any more.

I've seen a lot of people are exceptional at Oasis. They walk into a room and it just feels like everything will be okay. You know they're on their way over, and you know the problem will be solved. You can face difficulty during the day because you know at the end of the day you get to go home to your partner and get a hug and kiss to end your day.

A colleague had one of the worst nights of his life. He was a performer who had played to sold-out venues many times. He had been out of circulation for a while. He made his triumphant return with a heavily promoted comeback concert at a 500-person venue in San Diego. It turned into a disaster. His refuge that night was his mom. He called her on the phone because he knew that while mom can't fix anything, she can help him feel better.

We can be that kind of mother, father, friend… we can be Oasis for someone.

I AM A REFUGE

Here's the trick of having a Refuge: BE a Refuge.

I've coached people through this process. One of the saddest things I see is when someone demands Oasis, but they don't want to BE Oasis.

It's particularly bad when one person is on offense and gets upset when someone else defends. They want Oasis, they say, but what they really want is a lawful target. They don't want someone to share their day with as much as they want someone to take out their day on. That's not Oasis.

"Make the Relationship a Refuge" means everyone involved is part of the Oasis. It means everyone wins. It means everyone gives. It means people are safe because the place is safe and others are safe to talk to.

It means we seek resolution of differences rather than making others give up what they want so we can have what we want. It means we leave people better off than when they showed up in our lives. And if we can't help them, at least we don't hurt them.

PRACTICAL

Part of Oasis is the practical part. It is as simple as your presence leaves things better than you found them. If you're around, it's easier – easier to endure, easier to do – just easier all around. One of the things I tell the kids is that when they move out, their parents should have more work to do at the house - not less.

I learned that from my mother when I moved out. She had more things to do because I did more work around the house than my presence created. When I left, there was more to do because I was gone. The biggest positive difference from my departure was that groceries lasted a whole lot longer.

OASIS

As part of Ohana, Oasis means your presence makes it better. Your presence makes it safer. Your presence lets someone drop their guard and still be safe. This gives them a place to relax, recharge, and really be a whole person. It gives them a break from that life-sucking desert that life can so often be.

Oasis is refreshing. Oasis is a life-giving refuge.

OASIS
Be a Refreshing Refuge.
1:      Leave No Trace; Better Than You Found It
2:      Be a Safe Person; Create a Safe Place
3:      Give to Givers Who Give
4:      Win/Win or No Deal
5:      Resolve (My, Your, Our), Concede (Trade Wins), Compromise

CHAPTER SIX SUMMARY

1. Oasis: Be a Refreshing Refuge

2. Make it Better Because You're There

3. To have a Refuge, be a Refuge.

4. Being a Refuge means your presence makes it easier. You can often tell by whether your presence or absence makes for more work or less work.

5. Give people a place to relax, recharge, and really be a whole person.

CHAPTER SEVEN

HARMONY

Embrace Infinite Diversity in Infinite Combinations Aimed at Greatness.

O-Oasis
H-HARMONY
A-Assertiveness
N-Nobility
A-Aloha

Marian was invited to Thanksgiving with my family.

She walked in and saw that we were having a huge Thanksgiving party. Lots of familiar faces from the extended ohana from Hawaii were there. She said hello to a few people and headed to the kitchen to see if she could help.

I saw her standing in the entry to the kitchen stunned. She was captivated by... something. I walked over to find out what.

"Look at that!" she remarked. Later she described it as a well-oiled machine, or like a professional sports team, or like a choreographed dance.

In the kitchen were six or eight Hawaiian women miraculously bringing food together. It was the experienced teamwork of women who knew just how to bring this kind of thing together. No one seemed to be giving orders, but everything was happening. Marian was ready to step in to help, but she didn't feel she was good enough to step in at that level of play!

Instead, she joined me and my team to set the table. The way my team came together was that I got out stacks of dishes and people from the party just sort of mysteriously appeared tableside to start setting the table.

Marian had never seen something like that before. To her, it was incredible.

It was an example of Harmony.

HARMONY

Harmony requires difference.

Sameness has great value. Many people find that the more "like me" others are, the easier it is to get along. It's when things are different that getting along is more challenging.

Getting along despite differences is fairly elementary harmony. The simple way is to leave the differences out.

Getting along when many of your views and interests are diametrically opposed is much more advanced. For some people, it's too challenging. Anyone can do it, though. It just takes practice. Like anything else you begin at the elementary level and work your way up.

We see Harmony all the time. In sports, team members play different positions and work toward a unified goal. In music, band members play different instruments and deeply move audiences. In a choir, a collection of voices sings different notes, sometimes-different words, and brings a beautiful song into being.

In a business, a collection of different people work together to make business happen. There are the high profile people and the front-line people we might see, and behind the scenes there are unknown numbers making things happen. Take out any important piece, even if it's invisible, and the whole thing falls apart.

INFINITY

Here's a key idea behind Harmony: Infinity.

When sameness is the only way of working together, all you can do is look for others who are "like me." Then you gather as many "like me" people as you can with similar strengths, similar weaknesses, similar thinking, and similar blind spots. When this happens, there is a tendency for weaknesses and blind spots to amplify. The only real difference here is numbers.

Similar to sameness is "counterpart." Counterpart is "the other piece" of something. It's the pitcher and the catcher, the quarterback and the receiver, the man and the woman... you get the idea. Here, you start to get into teamwork. You gather together with varying strengths and weaknesses to fill in gaps. You start to play different positions to complete the team. Now you're starting to get some pretty impressive things done.

One version of this is task-oriented. You find people who can do particular tasks and you gather and assign tasks and team-projects get done as tasks are complete. At home, this could be an agreement on who does what chores at home.

Another version is role-oriented. You find people to fulfill roles, but the details of the tasks to be fulfilled is left more and more to the one who occupies the role. This creates many more options than division of task-lists. Now the individuals occupying those roles have job-descriptions, maybe key-performance-indicators, but how they get them done is largely up to them.

In one's personal life, you have roles and goals. You may have the role of husband or wife, father or mother, friend... whatever role you might fill, whatever label you might put to your role, and you do it. In some parts of life and business, you might have a tremendous amount of control over how you define your role.

The possibilities are already nearly endless. When you consider how many ways an individual might do a role, and how that might blend with how even just one other individual does their role, there are a lot of different ways to do it.

The more you involve more and more of the whole-person in whatever kind of team you're on, the more the possibilities approach infinity.

This is how we describe it:

"Embrace Infinite Diversity in Infinite Combinations Aimed at Greatness."

Embrace

"Embrace" means we take the fact there are differences as a good thing. It's good that we're not all the same. It's good that some of us are good at some things and some of us are good at other things. Note that this does NOT mean that every difference is a good difference. It only means that the fact there are differences is good. We embrace that. We celebrate it!

Infinite Diversity

"Infinite Diversity" means there are no limits on how different people might be. Sometimes we notice things like sex, but there are all sorts of ways females do "woman" and males do "man." We may notice race. For some people it's core to their identity, and for some it's incidental. Even when it's core to their identity, what that means also has great diversity. It's the same with religion. Not all Christians agree on all things. If you even split hairs down to an individual congregation, not every member of any given church agrees 100% with every other member of the very same church!

Then there's Infinite Diversity in skills, skill sets, education, what books someone has read, social views, values and value hierarchies, life experiences, relationship experiences, opportunities, goals dreams… it's amazing! There are no limits to how people can be uniquely them!

Infinite Combinations

"Infinite Combinations" means all these people with all these differences can come together in endless ways. You never know what's possible with the right group of people.

Serendipity is a sort of "happy accident" that can happen when a unique combination creates some wonderful adventure no one would have thought of on purpose!

Synchronicity is when "coincidence" produces a meaningful result. It is nearly impossible to plan either one.

Aimed at Greatness

"Aimed at Greatness" is intentional. It's when different people come together with a common aim – something you could call Greatness. This is always positive. It's something worthy. End results benefit many and hurt no one - or as few as possible.

We Do Not Have to Be Alike to Be Together

Harmony reminds us that we do not have to be alike to be together.

It's the differences that make things interesting. It's our differences that allow us to form better teams. In fact, differences are necessary to from synergized teams! We need people with strengths where we have weaknesses. We need counterparts. We need differences.

We can be different and still get along. That's an important part of Ohana.

HARMONY
Embrace Infinite Diversity in Infinite Combinations Aimed at Greatness.
1:    Just Be Polite
2:    More For, Less Against.
        Focus on What You Do Want.
3:    Facet Truths: Bring Truth
        Appropriate to the Relationship
4:    Differences are Issues to Navigate,
        Not Causes for Condemnation
5:    Bad Things are Problems to Solve,
        Not Causes for Condemnation

CHAPTER SEVEN SUMMARY

1. Harmony: Embrace Infinite Diversity in Infinite Combinations Aimed at Greatness

2. Infinity. If we're all the same, a team only varies by number. Counterparts are necessary partners to make work possible (pitcher/catcher). We can vary on tasks, on roles, and we approach infinity the more we form teams of whole-people.

3. Embrace means we take the fact of difference as good news. It makes synergy possible.

4. Infinite Diversity means there is no limit to how unique people can be.

5. Infinite Combinations means every time we take unique individuals and we team with one or more unique individuals, we form potentially limitless possible teams.

6. Aimed at Greatness means there's something great you're building together that is more than you can build alone.

7. We Do Not Have to Be Alike to Be Together

CHAPTER EIGHT

ASSERTIVENESS

Moving Forward On Purpose with Respect for Others.

O-Oasis
H-Harmony
A-ASSERTIVENESS
N-Nobility
A-Aloha

It was time to make a decision.

Yes, Mark was a friend, but he wasn't getting the job done. The project was falling apart and there was a lot at stake. If this project went bad, it could completely wipe us out.

My emotions ran strong. Anger said to fire Mark since he didn't accomplish what he said he'd accomplish. Fear said to cancel the whole project and run, surrendering the property to the bank and hope we'd survive.

If I was going to be assertive, I had to get centered and make clear-headed decisions. I waited until I was emotionally settled before I went to the property. If my emotions were still high, I'd be more aggressive and less assertive. I admit getting centered on that one took a lot.

I showed up to inspect the project and talk to Mark about where we were. He tried to paint a pretty picture, but when you dug behind the stories, the numbers were clear. We were losing more than seven thousand dollars a month.

This was my measured response. I told him I was putting the property up for sale. I did not know how long it would take to find a buyer. However long that was, to a limit of ninety-days, he could work the project. If he got it to break-even, just break-even, I would take it off the market.

In the months that followed, I helped him with signage, lead generation, and got him a team for property maintenance and upgrade. The work on the property served the dual-purpose of helping the project and helping the sale.

Mark's time ran out. In less than 60 days, we got an offer. The project was not at break-even. In fact, he had barely made any headway at all. We set up a long escrow so he'd have time to wrap up and the new owners would have time to set up.

Even then, I showed up in the last couple of weeks of escrow to make sure everything was being cleaned out okay. It wasn't. I got members of other teams to come help and we got done in 72 hours what had been taking Mark a month. The project was done, and Mark and I went our separate ways.

I learned to not get involved in any more projects with Mark. Yet I still consider him a friend. He has exceptional character just as I've known for years. But he lacked the competence for a job like this. Character and competence are two different things. That was an expensive lesson.

He's still a friend. The falling apart of the business partner role is separate from the friend role. I had a decision to make, and he understands that. He was in over his head, and I understand that. I made an assertive decision that looked after higher values, took care of my family, gave him a fair shot, and showed respect to everyone involved.

That is just one way to be assertive.

Assertiveness means to Move Forward On Purpose with Respect for Others.

Forward

"Move Forward" means you have a "forward." You've chosen something. You're moving toward something higher and better. It can be as simple as forward movement toward a specific goal. It can be pursuit of a larger mission. It can be more spiritual, the pursuit of some high ideal such as "family" or "love" or "self-respect."

A key to note here is that not everyone will agree on what is "forward." Something called "Miles Law" says: "Where you stand depends upon where you sit." What looks "forward" to one person might not be forward to someone else.

What is "forward" also depends upon one's particular focus. Sometimes things conflict, such as pursuit of career and relationship with family. One may require more time at work, while the other requires more time at home.

This is part of why "on purpose" is also important.

On Purpose

"On Purpose" has two meanings. One is intentional, that you've decided to do it so you're doing it. The second is that there is a higher purpose to it. There are concrete values being pursued or some ideal.

The better we understand what we consider "forward" and what our intended purpose is, the better we can evaluate. When we see what purpose we're fulfilling, we can also understand differing perspectives. For instance, if we're being assertive in our business and career goals, we may realize we're being passive in our family. It helps us live as a whole person more assertively.

Respect

"Respect for others" is the biggest difference between "assertive" and "aggressive." Aggressiveness tends to look at people as obstacles, opponents, or tools. Assertive looks at others as whole people who have intrinsic value. It sees that people have their own roles to fulfill and their own goals they are pursuing.

LIVE ASSERTIVELY

We Live Assertively. This means we decide what we choose for life to look like and we pursue that. A great deal of life is driven by circumstances. We must respond. It's just how things go. Even when we are in response-mode, we still get to decide how we choose to respond and how we'll adapt to what is.

Then there also much of life that is entirely up to us. Living Assertively means we take full responsibility and, where we can and should, we take control.

We Learn Assertively. This means we decide what to learn and we learn it. We might decide to learn that which is assigned to us, learning academic subjects, learning jobs, and learning skills for our job.

We can also choose what else to learn, choosing books to read, choosing audios to listen to, choosing seminars to attend, and choosing classes to enroll in.

We Love Assertively. This is often a mind-bender for people who think love should "just happen." It means we learn what love is (we'll discuss it more under Aloha) and we choose to practice it.

ASSERTIVE PRACTICES

We practice Assertive Listening. This means we seek to understand. We'll listen, ask clarifying questions to make sure we understand, and reflect back our understanding. We'll try to understand what someone means by what they say, defining terms, and giving the benefit of the doubt to our communication partner.

We practice Assertive Relationships. This means we learn how relationships work and we invest in them. The entire book is substantially about Assertive Relationships, but look particularly at Chapter 36: 100 Ways to Win: YORI.

We practice Assertive Leadership. This means we lead in a way that has a forward and is respectful. Most of this book impacts leadership, but look particularly at Chapter 29: 360-Degree Leadership: 4P360.

We practice Assertive Parenting. There's a lot in parenting that is known. We know babies will need to be fed, clothed, and housed. We know children need to learn language and get their basic education. We know they need to learn to live in civilized society.

Then there's about 20% of parenting that is just chaos. We may not have any answers (which is rough on parents), but we do our best. The more we have a vision for our children that respects who they are as individuals, the easier it is to deal with the chaos. At least we have a starting point!

ASSERTIVENESS

Assertiveness is distinct from aggressiveness. Aggressiveness is "moving without respect for others." Note that it lacks the "forward" since when aggressiveness flows from selfishness, bitterness, or anger, the movement is often not forward. It might be forward, but it might be sideways (it just changes things without making them better or worse), or it might be backwards. Also, there is often no higher purpose. And the respect for others is lacking. In fact, sometimes it's active disrespect for others.

Assertiveness is a virtue. Aggressive is rarely so (some circumstances call for it, but not many). By having cleaner definitions of what we mean, we can Live Life Assertively.

ASSERTIVENESS
Moving Forward on Purpose with Respect for Others.
1: I Have a Point; You May Also Have a Point
2: More Yes/And, Less No/But
3: Define Your Win: Values, Goals, and Roles
4: Compelling Future: Choose. Plan. Check In
5: Ecology Check

CHAPTER EIGHT SUMMARY

1. Assertiveness: Moving Forward On Purpose With Respect for Others

2. Forward is something you choose intentionally as forward. Others may disagree with you as to whether that's forward or not, and that's okay.

3. Purpose has two meanings.
    a. You have made your choice and move with intention.
    b. You have higher values you're pursuing.

4. Respect looks at others as whole-people with intrinsic value.

5. Living Assertively means we take full responsibility and, where we can and should, we take control.

6. Assertive Practices include things like Assertive living, loving, learning listening, assertive relationships, assertive leadership, and assertive parenting.

7. Assertive is distinct from Aggressive
    Assertive has a chosen forward designated as forward movement. Aggressive might move, but upon reflection, the movement was not always forward.
    Assertive has a higher purpose. Aggressive often expresses a desire, but is not always focused on higher ideals.
    Assertive shows respect for others as people. Aggressive tends to see people as obstacles to be overcome.

CHAPTER NINE

NOBILITY

Royal Knight: Be our highest and best selves.

O-Oasis
H-Harmony
A-Assertiveness
N-NOBILITY
A-Aloha

I lived at home and attended a university I could see from my bedroom window. My friends had gathered for our weekly game time. There were six of us hanging out downstairs at my mother's house.

We were into our game when my mother came downstairs. "I need help!" she said. "One of the neighbor ladies up the street had a pipe burst, her husband is out of town, and we need help up there!"

The team of six young men instantly mobilized. We headed up the street with my mother to the house of a woman none of us had ever met. The water had already been turned off, so it was mostly heavy lifting and cleaning up water. In a couple of hours we had everything off the floor, most of it outside, the water cleaned up, and everything was safe – for now.

She would still need to call a plumber to fix the burst pipe and a service to come dry out her carpets and see to her walls, but the immediate problem was handled. None of us knew her. To these six young men she was simply a damsel in distress, a lady my mother's age, and she needed help.

For these six young men, it felt a little extra cool that we were helping a lady. To be honest, though, we would have helped anyone. That's what we did.

That's how this particular group of friends operated. Some people wonder where such young men and women are today. Frankly, I see them all the time everywhere. I see it in men and women, in young and old, and across all demographics.

It's much more common than we sometimes realize.

KNIGHT IN SHINING ARMOR

The "knight in shining armor" ideal reminds us to face life with the courage of a knight heading toward battle. Problems, challenges, and crises are dragons to be slain. Goals are treasures to be won.

Sometimes it shows up in ways very much related to potential combat.

They heard a woman screaming. Two young men and a young woman headed out from to see where it was coming from. It was near. A man was yelling. A door slammed hard, and it got quiet. Then they heard her crying.

They went to the house with all the noise and heard the cries at a window on the side. The layout was just like another house they knew, so they got near that window and could tell that a woman was there by herself. They asked if everything was okay. She said no. She asked if they could call the police. She was safe for now, but she really wanted the police there before he came anywhere near her again.

The three neighbors called the police. Then they lingered nearby out of line-of-sight from the house. They had a plan to go in to help her only if there was immediate danger. One of them would engage the man and try to calm things down. The young lady would get the woman to safety. The third would be the buffer in between.

Fortunately, as hoped for and expected, the police arrived. Everyone relaxed. They acted wisely. They were prepared to act bravely. That's knightliness.

That is particularly important to me because my very first contact with death was the murder of a family friend. She was heard screaming for help in the middle of the night. No one came. No one so much as called the police. The killer was never found.

You can imagine I appreciate those with the level of knightliness to be ready and willing to help. I likewise appreciate the wise restraint shown so they did not escalate the situation. I wish my friend would have had neighbors like that.

ROYAL KNIGHT

The ideals of the Royal Knight blend royalty with knightliness.

"Princess" sometimes has competing meanings. Some take it as an entitled, self-absorbed, demanding woman. Of course, that's not what we mean here. Others take it as something wonderful. Obviously that's what we mean.

We draw on the definition of Ohana popularized by Disney. We also draw on the Disney-style princess. Think about them. There's beauty, grace, and kindness in the classic princesses. There are the smarts of Belle, the resilience of Pocahontas, the hard work of Tiana, and the leadership of Jasmine. Of course there are the kind of limitations and stereotypes you'd expect in children's movies of the time each Disney film was made, but each princess has virtue and we focus there.

Then, of course, there are other princesses. Wonder Woman is the Princess Diana. There's Xena, the warrior princess. With Disney, Mulan is a soldier, Merida is a master-archer, and Moana shows courage, insight, and a willingness to risk it all for her people – even standing up to the gods.

We have precious few popular Prince characters to draw upon for specific examples. They tend to be more two-dimensional than the women, but they are routinely brave, willing to risk for what's right, for duty, and for love.

For our purposes, royalty is also about leadership. It's about taking responsibility to be a leader. The more you learn about the leadership system 4P360, the more you realize that you are a leader everywhere. The average person touches the lives of 20,000 people over the course of a lifetime. Whether a moment with a cashier, or a lifelong relationship with family or friends, how we touch those lives means something.

Knightliness combines modern concepts of chivalry and the samurai concept of bushido. It's about courtesy, fairness, and courage. It's about being a gentleman or a lady, and knowing when it's important to do it and when it is best set it aside. Diving in to both chivalry and bushido as it applies today is a powerful metaphor for living.

"Highest and Best Self" is self-evident for some people and a confusing concept for others.

Consider that one of the highest ideals in life is love. When you feel love for others, when it's really powerful, when love overflows your heart, what does it look like in you? The kind of love you might feel early in a romance often inspires great things in us. The kind of love we have at engagement or marriage also does it. So does that moment when we first fall in love with our newborn child. Almost universally, that bright, shining, glowing feeling of love inspires us to our highest and best selves.

Another high ideal is joy. Yes, it's true that many people do all sorts of "not so high and not so best" things in pursuit of pleasure or happiness. But think about the other side of that. What do we do when we're at our happiest? What do we do when we're most joyful? When that special kind of happiness bubbles up from somewhere within, what are we like? When we're already happy, what do we do? That's often from our highest and best self.

Think of what kind of person you are when you're at your most peaceful. When you feel most centered. When life feels in balance. Think about where you are in life in those moments of abundance. When you feel like there's plenty for everyone and a lot of it is coming to you and through you, what are you like?

Most of us get an idea of our highest and best self somewhere in these examples, maybe in all of them. The goal is to bring that person to our Ohana as often as possible.

NOBILITY

Royal Knight: Be our highest and best selves.

1:     Inspired Action from Emotional Insight
2:     Be a Light, Not a Judge
3:     Self-Leadership
4:     360 Degree Leadership: 4P360
5:     Living By a Code

CHAPTER NINE SUMMARY

1. Nobility: Royal Knight: Be Our Highest and Best Self

2. The "knight in shining armor" ideal reminds us to face life with the courage of a knight heading toward battle. Problems, challenges, and crises are dragons to be slain. Goals are treasures to be won.

3. The ideals of the Royal Knight blend royalty with knightliness.

4. Royalty is about leadership. It's about taking responsibility to be a leader.

5. Highest and Best Self. For some, this is self-evident. For others, it can be confusing. Consider who you are when you're motivated by love, joy, and/or peace. Most of us get an idea of our highest and best self somewhere in these.

CHAPTER TEN

ALOHA

O-Oasis
H-Harmony
A-Assertiveness
N-Nobility
A-ALOHA

When I was six, I had my first martial art lesson. Over the years, I did Little League, some soccer, and in high school, I was a jumper in track. You'll notice there's no football.

As an adult, I was never much into sports. I might enjoy the occasional live baseball game. If a team I cared about was in an important game, I might watch. Over the years, on any given Super Bowl Sunday I would probably not be watching. I'd more likely be somewhere enjoying the lack of crowds.

I have a rule. If I love you and it's important to you, it's important to me because it's important to you. So when I had a son in football, suddenly football became important to me. I got tickets to an NFL game and took him.

Since I was going there to enjoy the game because I enjoy him, I warned him that I might have a lot of questions as we go. I understand the basics, but that's about it. I make a point to really enjoy these times because I really am there to connect with someone who matters to me.

As it worked out, he also got to witness me in action. There was a drunk who was picking fights with fans of both teams. My step-son said he was silently wondering if I was going to do anything about it, and I did. Quietly. Using pressure points, subtle control techniques, and de-escalation techniques. So far, he's the only current student who's actually seen first-hand what I'm like in those situations. That was an extra bonus on the specialness of the day.

I tell this story rather than a story of romantic love or commitment-through-crisis because I think it illustrates the simple every-day-ness of Aloha. Thanks to romantic movies, books, poetry and love songs, I think we have a pretty good idea of that kind of more spectacular love. Love is all those wonderful, grand, heart-stirring things. It is also the quiet, simple, every-day nature of loving connection with others.

A BASIC DEFINITION OF LOVE

"Love" is such a flexible word in English. We might use it for our child, our spouse, our sweetheart, or our parent. We could use the exact same word for a favorite pizza, drink, or a ride at Disneyland. We use the word to express devotion and commitment. We use the word to express attraction, desire, or even selfish possessiveness.

So this word would probably benefit from a definition. Here's the one we use as a basic definition of love for Ohana.

Love:
1. I want the best for you.
2. I want to be the best for you.
3. I want you to have transcendent joy.

This is such a simple, three-part definition that I've taught it to children. Six year-olds get it. I also teach it to pre-teens before they hit dating age. I want them to know the difference between people who really love them and who say "love" and mean "desire."

The "best" parts of it are compass headings. There is no singular best for all people at all times. There isn't even a best for one person that lasts a lifetime. Best is a compass heading that gives us a direction. When we discover better than what is, we want it for someone.

For ourselves, it's good to evaluate how we connect with people. While we define love in terms of what we want for others, it shows up in action. In that sense, love is a verb.

MANY FACETS OF LOVE

Having a basic definition of love lets us know what we're talking about. Love is such a powerful subject that is so central to our lives that it's worthy of thought and study. So we have more!

Love shows up in all sorts of ways. To put it in general categories, we create a love stack. That's a whole lesson unto itself, and the subject of Chapter 32.

Agape (a-GAH-pay) is unconditional love. This is character-based. It flows from who you are. If you want a very good definition of this kind of love you'll find it in the Bible at 1 Corinthians 13:4-8. Don't have a Bible handy? You can find that famous love passage at nearly any gift store. It starts "Love is patient, love is kind…"

Phileo (FIL-ee-oh) is conditional love. This is relationship-based. It flows from the interactions between the people in the relationship. The more you have positive interaction, the more positive you feel about the person. The more you have negative interactions, the more negative you feel. The important thing to know here is that negative is much more powerful than positive. It's easier to break things than it is to build things.

(I admit that while the proper pronunciation is FIL-ee-oh, I tend to pronounce it fil-AY-oh because that's how I first learned it. It also reminds the listener that I'm talking about my whole teaching on the subject.)

Eros (ee-ROS), the way I use it, is Experience or Sensation. More technically, it is the sexual component of romantic love. Using that as a model, we focus on the fact that it is the intense feelings we get with experiences that produce powerful sensations. (This is another I first learned technically incorrect and stick with my way so it's clear I'm talking about my teaching here.)

Outside the stack we have Storge (STOR-gay), or family love. This is the particular affection you tend to have for someone to whom you are related. Often, it shows up in that we give people we're related to a higher automatic starting point for relationship. We also tend to put up with more without ending the relationship.

HELLO AND GOODBYE

Aloha also means hello and goodbye. We apply it as the simple act of greeting someone when you see them and saying goodbye when you leave. Depending upon the relationship, that might include a handshake, a hug, and/or a kiss. It could include walking someone out and seeing them off.

A simple understanding is a loving hello and a fond farewell.

On a deeper level, it also means "no ghosting." We used to call it dumping. It's the act of disappearing on someone without telling them it's over. The simple part of aloha meaning goodbye means you don't just vanish. You break up. You say goodbye.

BE CONSISTENTLY LOVING

Love is a verb. That means it can be a habit. By practicing it consistently, we get better at it. We make it a habit so that we are consistently, habitually loving! That's the goal.

We live a life of love. People know they can count on us to be a loving person. They know that we'll be in relationship with them with the Aloha Spirit.

ALOHA
Love:
1. I want the best for you.
2. I want to be the best for you.
3. I want you to have transcendent joy.
　　1:　　Love Stack: Agape, Phileo, Eros
　　2:　　Love Is & Love Is Not: A Self-Check
　　3:　　Phileo Bank Account: Positive On Purpose
　　4:　　Love, Joy, Peace; God, People, Self
　　5:　　100 Ways to Win: YORI

CHAPTER TEN SUMMARY

1. Aloha: Love

2. Basic Definition: Love:
    1. I want the best for you.
    2. I want to be the best for you.
    3. I want you to have transcendent joy.

3. "Best" is a compass heading. There is no singular best for all people at all times.

4. Love has many facets. It appears in many forms.

5. Agape – Unconditional Character-Based Love

6. Phileo – Conditional Relationship-Based Love

7. Eros – Situational, Experience-Based Love

8. Storge – Family Love

9. Aloha also means Hello and Goodbye. Think of a loving hello and a fond farewell.

10. Be Consistently Loving.

CHAPTER ELEVEN

INTRODUCING OHANA INTO YOUR ORGANIZATION

My Ohana stories slide between those I've been Ohana for, those who have been Ohana for me, and stories of clients. Ohana behavior is so common in my life that people are sometimes shocked when it doesn't happen.

Even so, we're not perfect. As you try to do Ohana, you'll find that you're not perfect at it – no matter how long you practice. Neither is anyone else. You'll get better. So will they – if they're working at it.

There's a lot here. As quickly as we've covered Oasis, Harmony, Assertiveness, Nobility, and Aloha here, it's still a lot. The dive into the five-by-five makes for a total of thirty chapters to study. Even then, the study just scratches the surface.

You can go far, far deeper if you like.

On the flip side, you can also start light. If you want to introduce the idea of Ohana to your group or organization, begin with *The Ohana Way Fundamentals*. That book is this book, except much shorter. It lacks the twenty-five chapters of the five-by-five. It makes for much faster reading. It's less of a stretch for most people's thinking.

STARTING LIGHT: THE OHANA WAY FUNDAMENTALS

In *The Ohana Way Fundamentals*, we just touch on the surface level of OHANA. We talk about Oasis, Harmony, Assertiveness, Nobility, and Aloha. As noted at the end of each chapter, there are five areas for a deeper dive under each of them. That's The Ohana Five-by-Five.

We've made the deeper dive in *The Ohana Way 2.0*, so you've got Ohana coming in loud and clear. The signal is strong. (The five-by-five metaphor is originally from radio broadcasts, if you didn't already know and have forgotten from earlier in the book.)

Defining Ohana clearly (defining anything clearly, for that matter) helps us have conversations when something isn't quite right. It provides for starting points when you're building something new. It provides individual elements as you go.

The power of *The Ohana Way 2.0* is that it provides the 25 important concepts that enhance and enrich the core five ideals of Ohana. By exploring the subject in more depth, you can find places that may need more attention. You can choose to focus on one thing at a time.

For instance, if you were to bring *The Ohana Way* into a business environment, you might start something as simple an introduction, yet powerful, as Hero, Villain, Victim. Then move to the basics of "family" and "no one gets left behind" and "no one gets forgotten" for the first few weeks.

Breaking inertia can take effort. You may already find that you have some tough conversations needed. If you're the leader, it's best to have already read the whole book and gotten into 4P360 and YORI a bit. That way you're ready if team members bring up difficult things.

While it's in my best interests to sell you more books and programs, I would start with *The Ohana Way Fundamentals*.

First, it's inexpensive. Before you invest too much getting too deep, start with the report. It's a very solid start, and the report is short enough that it's not at all intimidating. No one will hold a copy of the report in their hands and wonder when the heck they'll ever have time to read something so thick. It's short. It's quick. It's inexpensive.

Second, you can get a very good sense of whether you have resistance to the idea. Depending upon the nature of your team's culture, Ohana might be an easy fit... or not so easy a fit. Depending upon what you do and how you do it, you might find that your people just aren't interested.

LEADERS GO FIRST

My experience shows that a lack of interest in this usually means that they don't trust it. If the team doesn't trust the leadership because of the "program of the month" syndrome or "buzzword of the year" syndrome, then, to them, it's just one more program for the sake of a program, and they don't expect anything from it. If that's the case, the solution is simple: Leaders Go First.

The other form of not trusting it is if team members think that leadership is doing this as some sort of manipulation. If leaders either have a demonstrated history of not respecting team members as whole people, the distrust might be warranted. It might take some time to earn that trust. In this case, the solution is also simple: Leaders Go First. (You notice there's a theme here.)

There is a need for leaders to go first, then the team members can have the report for their own edification while the leadership goes through *The Ohana Way 2.0* or one of my Ohana Programs. *The Ohana Way Fundamentals* will give the team enough to know what's going on so they can watch the leaders and see for themselves.

There's a very good chance that *The Ohana Way* will be very appealing to any team of people. Whether you're in a small group or a large organization, the ideals of Ohana are attractive – for those who believe it can be real. Certainly I've seen it be real!

In that case, *The Ohana Way 2.0* and *The Ohana Programs* together are powerful. Or one or the other. Or have me in for live training. Or combine them in any way that serves your organization.

You've read *The Ohana Way 2.0*. Just imagine if you had more Ohana in your life. Imagine getting up in the morning with your home-Ohana, heading off to spend the day working with your work-Ohana, heading to your martial arts school to train with your dojo-Ohana, and then back home to your home-Ohana.

What a life that would be! And you can be a part of making that true by starting with this simple admonition: Be Ohana!

CHAPTER ELEVEN

1. Introduce Ohana Intro Your Organization
    a. Begin with Hero, Villain, Victim
    b. Then Ohana, "family," and "no one is left behind," and "no one is forgotten."

2. Starting Light: *The Ohana Way Fundamentals*
    Begin with Ohana: Oasis, Harmony, Assertiveness, Nobility, Aloha

3. Then move on to the Ohana 5x5

4. Leaders Go First

5. Start with this simple admonition: Be Ohana!

EPILOGUE

This concludes my 30th Anniversary edition of The Ohana Way.

We covered a lot of ground.

In 2019, I closed down my San Diego GKKD Martial Arts Dojo. We had what we called an End Of An Era party. My leaders and students got together and gifted me with a journal. In that journal, many of my students – current and former – wrote me notes.

Guardian Kempo Kajuko Do is a very comprehensive martial art. We have a proven self-defense track record stretching back to 1990. It includes striking, grappling, and weapons. We have fourteen years of curriculum. Curiously, NONE of that was part of the notes.

They all talked about Ohana. They talked about the dojo feeling like home. They talked about the dojo family as family. That's what was really important to them.

I would not have guessed that the place they all come to learn martial arts would be so important not because of the martial art – but because of the Ohana. But that explains why Ohana got so much attention years ago when it was my Ohana that rescued me.

I had plans to be in Las Vegas for two weeks. There was a martial arts convention across a few of the days. I didn't have any staff or a leadership team. Years earlier, I had a team of 14 with me. In this year, a couple of colleagues had joined me, and, of course, I had a lot of colleagues and friends in town.

It was the end of the first week. I was on a date. I'd gone to the Wynn and enjoyed a drink with some lovely company on the patio at the Wynn Resort. I enjoyed the Lake of Dreams show. Because I didn't already know this lady, I didn't look at my phone. After our date, I headed back to my car.

Looking at my phone, I discovered that Jamar had been trying to get hold of me. I had texts, Facebook messages, phone calls and messages, video calls, audio messages... more than a dozen tries across all connections. Rather than check those messages, I thought I should just call him back.

He told me a car had crashed into my business. He sent photos.

He was there. Deputy Sheriffs were there. The California Highway Patrol was there. The Fire Department was there. The County Building Inspector was there. Earlier, the Paramedics had been there and an ambulance had taken away the driver and passenger. For this hour in this neighborhood, it was the biggest thing going on.

I made one call to a black belt of mine that lived nearby. I just told her that I was entrusting her to make any decisions that might need to be made. In minutes, there were four people there, clients and some family-of-clients. I told the necessary authorities who I was and who had authority in my absence, and things started to happen.

I had overnight security. In the morning, new people arrived. Pictures were posted, and in the morning, without being asked, people started to show up to help. A news crew came by, and my clients talked to them, handled the interview and news team, and got them the photos.

I had a lunch date and some other appointments, but my friends saw the social media posts. I got messages and calls explaining that they totally understood that I had to go back to San Diego. I told them that I'd still make the meetings – because San Diego was under control. My clients had it handled. They told me to stay on vacation, so I did!

A friend of mine from out of town got hold of me. She saw on social media what had happened. As a fellow business owner, she could only imagine what it would be like to have your business location destroyed while out of town. When she found out that my clients were taking care of it all, she was astonished.

"How did that happen?" she wanted to know.

"They're my ohana."

"What's that?" she asked.

I explained that it was Hawaiian for family, and my clients were like family. They were taking care of it for me, and they told me to stay on vacation. I would go back in a week when originally scheduled. She said that sounded incredible, and she wanted to know if I had a system for that.

Of course I did. Ohana had been systemized for a while. When she saw the books and the programs, she decided she wanted to be a part of getting the word out.

Twenty-four hours after a car crashed into my storefront, it was all cleaned up and boarded up. Classes resumed on Monday right on schedule while I was still gone.

How did that happen?

Be Ohana.

Build Ohana.

Bring Ohana to the World.

Made in the USA
Monee, IL
18 December 2020